ANN GRIFFITHS

AND HER WRITINGS

LLEWELLYN CUMINGS

SLG Press

Convent of the Incarnation Fairacres
Parker Street Oxford OX4 1TB England

www.slgpress.co.uk

First published by SLG Press, 2012

© LLEWELLYN CUMINGS, 2012

Cover illustration:

© Chris Derricott, 2012: *Original photograph of sheep near Llanfihangel, a few miles from the birthplace of Ann Griffiths*

ISBN: 978-0-7283-0201-3
ISSN: 0307-1405

Excerpts from Hymns and Letters, Ann Griffiths, *trans. by Alan Gaunt & Alan Luff,* © 1999, Stainer & Bell, 23 Gruneisen Road, London N3 1DZ. *www.stainer.co.uk Reproduced with permission.*

Printed by:
Will Print Oxford England

CONTENTS

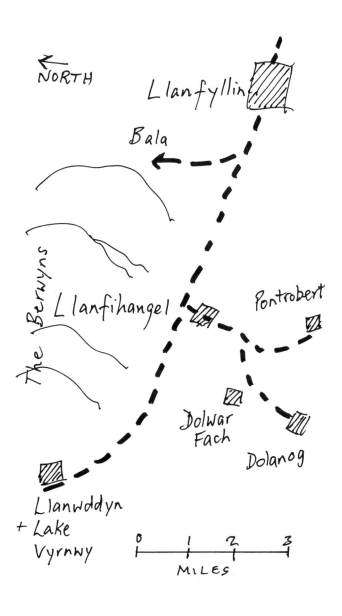

NORTH

Llanfyllin

Bala

The Berwyns

Llanfihangel

Pontrobert

Dolwar Fach

Dolanog

Llanwddyn
+ Lake
Vyrnwy

0   1   2   3
MILES

Map of the area

iv

INTRODUCTION

WALES has produced a multitude of singers, poets and writers of distinction. Amongst these is Ann Griffiths, a young woman who was born in 1776 and who lived in a remote corner of north-east Wales. She died in 1805, aged twenty-nine. In her lifetime she probably never travelled more than twenty-five miles from her home; yet the hymns she wrote are regarded as some of the most inspired in Welsh hymnody.

Ann lived at the end of the eighteenth and the start of the nineteenth centuries. It was a time of widespread religious and social change in Wales, affecting the lives of people even in remote corners of Montgomeryshire, where Ann Griffiths lived her short life. The ancient parish churches had long been the focus for the spiritual needs of the Welsh people; but the publication and availability of the Welsh Bible, translated by William Morgan and published in 1588, ignited the flame of personal conviction and evangelical faith. In 1689 Parliament passed the Act of Toleration, which allowed Dissenters to build their own places of worship. By Ann's time, education was beginning to reach all corners of Wales. The prevailing mood of religious seriousness, especially among the Welsh-speaking population, prepared people for the waves of spiritual renewal which flowed across Wales during Ann's lifetime.

From the small market town of Llanfyllin in north-east Montgomeryshire, a road leads over the foothills of the Berwyn mountains towards Lake Vyrnwy. Five miles along this road, on the crest of a high ridge on the left, there is an inconspicuous church. This is the parish church of Llanfihangel-yng-Ngwynfa ('the church of St Michael in a white place'. 'White place means here 'cleanness' or 'purity', and it is a reference to the beauty of the surrounding hills and valleys). This is the church where Ann Griffiths was baptised and married, where she is buried, and where her father was churchwarden.

1

the church at Llanfihangel-yng-Ngwynfa

Llanfihangel-yng-Ngwynfa is a small hamlet, typical of many in Montgomeryshire. Today, the surrounding rolling hills support mainly hill sheep-farmers, whose white farm-houses dot the landscape. The farmhouse, Dolwar Fach ('little meadow, dale'), in which Ann grew up is two and a half miles south of Llanfihangel, a short distance from the road between Llanfihangel and the hamlet of Dolanog. The original stone-built farmhouse is a long, low building. It is now a farm shed, and a newer farmhouse stands beside it. The buildings are unpretentious and are suggestive of the hard, demanding life of upland farmers in the Welsh hills. The rented farm of some eighty acres would, in Ann's day, have supported cattle, sheep, pigs and poultry; and potatoes, oats and barley would have been grown.

SUMMARY OF ANN'S LIFE

ANN GRIFFITHS was born in 1776 to John Evan Thomas, a tenant farmer, and his wife, Jane Thomas. She was fourth in a family of five children: John, Jane, Elizabeth, Ann and Edward. Theirs was a Welsh-speaking household, and Welsh was the language of worship in the parish church. The family was steeped in the cultural traditions of this part of Montgomeryshire, in which music and the composing of hymns and ballads were prominent. To this day, the eisteddfod and the *plygain* (the singing of locally-composed carols around the farmhouses at dawn on Christmas Day) still have popular support. Ann grew up in a respectable, hard-working farming family. As well as being churchwarden, John Thomas was for a time supervisor of the poor of the parish.

at the spinning wheel

Ann had some instruction in reading and writing Welsh from the curate at the church, and had English lessons for a time with Mrs Owen 'y Sais' ('the English woman') at Dolanog. Ann was a lively young woman who would walk miles to dances, and who enjoyed partying. In 1794, Ann's mother died. Ann, now aged eighteen, had to look after the running of the household, do her share of farm chores, and care for her father.

During the late eighteenth century the Welsh Methodist Revival was making inroads into north Wales, and meetings had already begun in Ann's area. At Bala, across the Berwyn mountains, large numbers gathered to listen to the preaching of Thomas Charles, an Anglican minister who whole-heartedly supported the cause of the Revival, and who later set up his own independent chapel. Ann, as a loyal Anglican, was dismissive of the crowds who flocked to hear him, commenting, 'There go the pilgrims on their way to Mecca.' To her dismay, her two brothers John and Edward were beginning to be influenced by, and to identify themselves with, the Revival movement.

In the summer of 1796, Ann was visiting her sister Jane at the corner shop in Llanfyllin. She and her cousin were on their way to a St David's Day dance at the farm in Pengorphwysfa in the hills above Llanfyllin. The local independent chapel of Pendref had invited the Reverend Benjamin Jones of Pwllheli to preach in the open air outside the Goat Inn (now the Cain Valley Hotel), just across the road from the corner shop in Llanfyllin. Ann overheard the preaching, which she found disturbing and thought-provoking. This marked the beginning of the spiritual search which led to her conversion.

Llanfyllin

4

Ann continued to attend her parish church, even though by now the rest of her family were worshipping with the new fellowships which were springing up. The following Christmas, Ann went alone, in some distress, to her church for the early morning service. After the service the minister, Thomas Evans, invited her to breakfast. During conversation, they discussed the Revival. The minister made some disparaging remarks about it, which dismayed Ann. She decided the time had come for her to follow her brothers and to seek spiritual enlightenment among the Methodists. She began to attend the house meetings in Dolanog and Pontrobert. Here, in an atmosphere of devotional prayerfulness, people read the Bible, shared their spiritual insights and experiences, and prayed for one another and their unconverted neighbours.

Llyn Tegid: the lake at Bala

Once a month Ann walked, either alone or with friends, five miles to the village of Llanwddyn (now submerged under Lake Vyrnwy), where she spent the night at the inn, and then walked another ten miles across the Berwyns to Bala, where Thomas Charles preached at his 'Communion Sundays'. Large crowds gathered for these inspirational gatherings. These long walks gave her time for reflection on what she heard.

in the Berwyns

As Ann penetrated more deeply into the Christian faith, she became increasingly in awe of its truths and began to give expression to her sense of wonder in stanzas of her own composition in Welsh. Sometimes she wrote on scraps of paper which were secreted under cushions on chairs. Other compositions were written down or memorised by Ruth Evans, the maid in the house. Some thirty of these survive in the form of hymns of several verses, or single stanzas. Ruth Evans supplied tunes for some of the hymns.

John Hughes, a prominent Methodist who supervised the 'circulating schools'—a system whereby itinerant teachers taught children in rural areas—lodged at Dolwar Fach for some months in 1799 and became Ann's spiritual counsellor. When he moved away, Ann kept in touch with him by letter, and poured out her thoughts on her own spiritual condition and that of her congregation in Pontrobert. John Hughes copied out seven of Ann's letters into a notebook. Only one letter in Ann's handwriting survives, a letter written to the sister of Ruth Evans, Elizabeth, who lived at Guilsfield, near Welshpool.

On 10 October 1804 Ann married a prominent Methodist farmer of Meifod, Thomas Griffiths, who has beeen described as a gentle and loveable man, in Llanfihangel church. Soon after, John Hughes married Ruth the maid at Llanfihangel, and Ann and Thomas were present as witnesses. On 13 July 1805 Ann gave birth to a baby daughter, Elizabeth, who survived only two weeks and was buried on 31 July. Ann herself lived only a few days longer and was buried on 12 August. Thomas Evans conducted both funeral services.

John Hughes brought Ann's hymns to the attention of Thomas Charles in Bala, and he published them in 1806. In 1846 John Hughes published a short biography of Ann in Welsh,[1] together with copies of some of her letters.

the farmhouse, Dolwar Fach

ANN'S HYMNS

THE HYMNS that Ann composed are regarded as one of the literary treasures of Wales. They are remarkable for their originality, precision, devotional intensity, Christ-centredness, and rich use of Bible imagery. Above all, her hymns and letters show to what a remarkable degree Ann experienced the love of God in Christ, and how she reciprocated that love with her whole heart. In her hymns, Ann expresses her orthodox Christian faith. The themes covered by her hymns can be said to be expositions of the main themes of the Christian Creed, themes which caused her worshipful wonder. At times Ann was so moved by what she saw that that she seemed to withdraw from this world altogether, to the neglect (she felt) of her worldly duties. As she meditated, she was in 'a sea of wonders'.[2] As to how inspiration came to her, one can only speculate. Partly, perhaps, it came from the preaching of Thomas Charles; partly from the shared insights of the group of believers in Pontrobert; but very largely, probably, from her own prolonged meditation during her time spent in Bible reading. In one of her letters she refers to 'visitations'—times of intense inner awareness. She spoke as she felt herself to be moved by the Holy Spirit.

In her hymns and letters, Ann is concerned with the relationship between human beings and Almighty God. This was no abstract, impersonal, academic issue for her; it involved her intimately. She wrote out of her own experience as a Christian, from the crucible of her own spiritual highs and lows.

Ann confronts the paradox of the two complementary sides to God's being: God's transcendence and holiness on the one hand, and God's grace and love in reaching out to humanity in Jesus Christ on the other. To Ann, God's holiness is dramatically shown by what happened at Sinai—the giving of the Law, austere and terrifying, by which all are judged and before which all stand condemned:

> Long ago, with Sinai blazing,
> when our God proclaimed his law,
> terrified their life was forfeit,
> sinners overwhelmed with awe,

Sinai was followed by the journey through the wilderness, during which God gave instructions for the building of the Tabernacle and the sacrificial arrangements which pointed forward to Calvary:

> at his feet, as mystery thundered,
> saw an altar set in place,
> where the offerings made foreshadowed
> one surpassing sacrifice.[3]

Ann's hymns refer frequently to the Law of God, a reflection of God's holiness, expressive of a standard of morality which is unattainable by mortals. The purpose of the Law is to convince us of sin—'apart from the law I had not known sin'[i]—and, in the mercy of God, to make us aware of our need of a Redeemer:

> Though the soul in greatest fervour
> blazes up with love's own fire,
> it can never scale the glory,
> God's pure law still reaches higher.[4]

All attempts to justify ourselves before God are futile:

> steadfast grace makes my case,
> in the futile fig-leaf's place![5]

Ann's awareness of the helpless plight of humanity, and her realization of her own sinfulness, are the preconditions for her amazement at God's redeeming work in Christ. She believes that God's Law must be honoured if we are to be reconciled to God. The only person who can fulfil this in its immensity is the Son of God, and he alone can make adequate atonement for our failure to keep it:

---

[i] Rom. 7: 7.

the law, in Jesus on the tree,
is fully satisfied.[6]

For Ann, the seeming contradiction of God's holiness—
God's transcendence and separateness—and mercy and grace
towards sinners finds a just resolution at the Cross. There
peace was made when Jesus voluntarily took upon himself
the sin of the world and suffered in our place.

Many of Ann's hymns are poems of praise in which she
exults in the wonders of the Incarnation, redemption and the
prospect of heaven, as in the hymn *Rhyfedd, rhyfedd gan
angylion*:

> Wonder! wonder to the angels,
> mighty wonder faith perceives:
> see life's giver and sustainer,
> ruler over all that lives,
> lying swaddled in a manger,
> with no resting place on earth,
> yet the shining host in glory
> now adores him at his birth.
>
> When Mount Sinai smokes and trembles,
> when the trumpet sounds on high,
> I can feast across the limit,
> and, in Christ the Word, not die;
> all the fulness dwelling in him
> fills perdition's emptiness,
> here the breach with God is mended,
> his self-sacrifice makes peace.[7]

Ann states clearly her belief in the deity of Jesus Christ. She
worships him, not only for what he did for all on the Cross,
but also for who he is.

It is possible that, during her Anglican upbringing, Ann
heard the Thirty-Nine Articles[8] in church. Article 2 declares:

> The Son, ... of one substance with the Father, took
> man's nature so that two whole and perfect Natures,

that is to say, the Godhead and the Manhood, were joined together in one Person, never to be divided.

Ann wrote in one of her hymns:

> O for the faith, with angels,
> to penetrate and see
> the plan of our salvation,
> its hidden mystery:
> two natures in one Person,
> conjoined inseparably,
> distinct and not confounded,
> in perfect unity.[9]

Ann's emphasis in her hymns is on Christ's redeeming work on the Cross. It is clear that in Ann's mind Jesus died as a substitutionary sacrifice for sin—her sin—and that through his death on the Cross she can approach God:

> Sinner is my name, most shameful,
> chief of all in sinfulness;
> yet such wonder! in this temple,
> finding God in quietness;
> he fulfils his law completely,
> the transgressor shares his feast,
> God and humans cry 'sufficient!'
> Jesus, Sacrificed, makes peace.
>
> Boldly, I will come before him;
> his gold sceptre in his hand,
> points toward this favoured sinner:
> here, accepted, all can stand.
> I'll press onward, shouting, 'pardon',
> fall before my gracious Lord:
> mine the pardon, mine the cleansing,
> mine the bleaching in his blood.[10]

Just as King Ahasuerus pointed his sceptre at Esther and

allowed her to approach the royal presence,[ii] so Jesus invites the penitent sinner into his presence.

Ann considers the death and burial of Jesus: Jesus, the source of all life, experiences death. But resurrection life moved in him, and God raised him triumphant :

> Source of peace, and peerless sovereign:
> see, my soul, where he was laid,
> —all creation moving in him—
> in the tomb, and with the dead;
> life of all the lost, their anthem,
> wonder to the seraphim;
> seeing God in flesh they worship,
> all in chorus, shout 'To Him!'[11]

During the Welsh Revival, congregations often cried out, 'To Him!'

Ann experienced turbulence to the depths of her being as she meditated on the immensity of Jesus' redeeming work. The sheer grace of God's forgiveness, acceptance and blessing through Christ moved her to tears: she often sat weeping at her spinning wheel, with her Bible open beside her. She struggled with her own inconstancy and sinfulness and her failure to keep close to Jesus. But she is reassured as she looks forward to the day when she will see him as he is. In Welsh congregations *Wele'n sefyll rhwng y myrtwydd* is one of her best-known and most-loved hymns:

> See him stand among the myrtles,
> object worthy of my mind,
> though I only partly know him,
> over all things, unconfined;
> hail that morning,
> when I see him as he is.[12]

The reference is to the messenger, the angel of the Lord, in the Book of Zechariah, who brings a message of hope to God's

[ii] Esther 4: 9-5; 3.

people.[iii] Ann identifies him with Jesus.

Ann prays for grace to prevent her faith growing cold:

> Must my zeal, like glowing embers,
> burning for your glory, Lord,
> kindness felt when I was younger,
> now go cold towards my God ?[13]

For the remainder of her earthly life she must keep to the Way—her life in Christ:

> Though it crosses human nature,
> this perplexing path I trace,
> I will travel on it calmly,
> while I see your precious face.[14]

She is not so preoccupied with her own spiritual life, however, as to lose concern for her fellow believers:

> O, my head should be all waters,
> weeping day and night away:
> Zion's army, with its banners,
> melts before the heat of day.[15]

Her eternal security depends not on her feeble grasp on Christ, but on his grasp of her, and the realization of God's purposes for his people:

> Comes the day the royal offspring
> gain their land across the sea;
> after slaving in the brickyards,
> share their Father's sovereignty;
> faith is there transformed to vision,
> hope becomes beatitude,
> where they sing faith's endless anthem,
> magnify the precious blood.[16]

Ann's hymns give full expression to the reality of conflict in the Christian life, but they look forward to the eventual

---

[iii] Zech. 1: 8-11.

13

triumph of Christ and his Kingdom. A note of praise and worshipful wonder is dominant:

> Shed this body of corruption,
> join the fervent choirs on high,
> there to penetrate the wonders:
> sure Salvation, Calvary;
> now I live to see the Unseen,
> he who died and lives as Lord,
> joined for ever, never parted,
> in communion with my God.[17]

Ann sings of the boundless resources of God's grace and love which are available to all believers, resources which flow from 'Bethesda's lake':

> In the waters of salvation,
> virtues flow continually;
> and within them gifts of healing,
> never failing, always free;
> sick ones from the fall of Eden,
> come and use these waters, take
> all their never ending virtues,
> substance of Bethesda's lake.[18]

> only resurrection's children
> swim in floods so deep and wide;
> fathomless and shoreless waters
> form Bethesda's mighty tide.[19]

She thinks longingly of heaven, where faith will turn to sight:

> There made perfect, in his image
> by whom God's atonement came,
> far beyond imagination,
> I will glorify his name;
> I will come into the mystery
> opened by his wounds, and then
> I will kiss the Son for ever,
> never turn from him again![20]

ANN'S LETTERS

OF ANN'S LETTERS, [21] seven written to John Hughes and one written to Elizabeth Evans of Guilsfield survive. They are intensely personal. In one of them, she thanks John Hughes for his letters, which carry reassuring messages for her:

> I have received your letters with affection, hoping that the weighty things that are in them will find place in my thought.[22]

Ann's letters deal mainly with her perception of her spiritual state, and to a lesser extent, the spiritual state of the congregation at Pontrobert. As she looks at her own life, she is ruthlessly perceptive and honest, but always finds reassurance in the promises of Scripture—'the pills of heaven'.

> I have had certain quite bruising trials, and strong winds, to the point that I was about to lose my breath on the hill path; but I believe that I was brought up to the top by the following two chains: 'And a Man shall be as a hiding place from the wind etc';[iv] and, 'Come, my people, enter thou into thy chambers, and shut the doors etc';[v] there was quiet and warmth for a while.[23]

> You know … my story in all kinds of misery.[24]

> The sin of the mind is what crushes me most heavily.[25]

Ann is particularly pained and ashamed by her ability to deceive the Pontrobert fellowship:

> I have recently been far gone in spiritual whoring away from the Lord; and yet holding up my head before the ministrations of the church as one who is keeping house well and remaining in the fellowship. But in spite of all my devices, the Lord broke upon me

[iv] Isa. 32: 2.
[v] Isa. 26: 20.

with these words: 'If I am a Father, where is my honour? If I am a Master, where is my fear?'[26]

In one of her letters, Ann expresses her uncertainty as to the authenticity of her inspiration, and looks to John Hughes for reassurance:

Beloved brother, I would be glad to see you many times in the midst of my distress of mind, suffering as I do gnawing doubts concerning the truth of the visitations, and the revelation of the Mediator, to a greater or lesser degree despite my damnable and lost state.[27]

She wrestles with the problem of the appeal of material things, things of this world which threaten always to supplant love of Christ as the supreme love of her life:

Dear brother, the thing that is most pressing on my mind at the present is the sin that any thing in this world of sight should take first place in my mind. I am reverently ashamed, and rejoice in astonishment, at the thought that the one for whom it is a condescension to behold the things that are in heaven, has given himself to be an object of love to a creature as base as I.[28]

Frequently Ann expresses her sense of wonder:

It is a wonder to me to think who it was upon the cross: the one whose eyes are as a flame of fire,[vi] piercing through the heavens and the earth, and at the same moment unable to see his creatures, the work of his two hands. My mind is drowning in too great an excess of wonder to say anything more on this.[29]

Ann acknowledges the mercy and grace of God shown to her, thanking God for the merciful, but just, interventions in her life:

[vi] Rev. 2: 18.

Thanks be for ever to the God of all grace for taking his precious word in his hand in his dealings with me: I reverently believe that so it is, and that his axes and their blows are continually upon the root of self-conceit that is so strong in my corrupt nature.[30]

My thought is that every idle word and all levity of spirit, and all behaviour that seems to be contrary to holiness, entirely denies that we know Jesus Christ. But in the face of our great wretchedness, how precious it is to think on that word: 'The Lord turned and looked upon Peter.'[vii] [31]

I am often at the throne of grace, in wonder, thanks and prayer: in wonder that the word and the Holy Spirit have found a way to treat the condition of such an unclean wretch, full of every deceit, without slaying me.[32]

Always, as she turns to Scripture, she finds reassurance and comfort. Her faith is securely in Christ Crucified, the great Mediator between God and humanity:

I am especially glad to think today on that word, 'And to Jesus, the Mediator of the New Covenant, and to the blood of the sprinkling':[viii] it is something new to love the teaching of the cleansing. That word is on my mind, 'the blood of Jesus Christ, his son, cleanseth us from all sin'.[ix] I had never a greater longing to be pure.[33]

Thanks be to God who is full of promises.[34]

In the midst of her turbulent thoughts, longings, sense of personal failure as a Christian, Ann finds peace at the Cross:

There was made plain to me more of my doomed condition some days ago than in the whole period of

[vii] Luke 22: 61.
[viii] Heb. 12: 24.
[ix] 1 John 1: 7.

my profession of faith, and more of the glory of the wise rule of God in justifying the godless, and that he is in Christ reconciling the world unto himself, not accounting their sins to them.[x] [35]

As Ann contemplates the future, and death itself, she writes to her friend Elizabeth Evans:

Dear sister, I see more need than I saw ever before to be able to spend what life is left to me in placing myself daily and continually, body and soul, into the care of him who is able to keep what is given to him until that day.[xi] Not giving myself once; but living in giving myself, until the time and at the time that I lay this tabernacle aside. … but I wait for the time to be freed, and be with Christ, for that is far better.[xii]

In the same letter Ann writes of her awareness—recently realised—of the significance of the indwelling Holy Spirit:

Beloved sister, the subject most special on my mind at the present concerns grieving the Holy Spirit. That word came to my mind, 'Know ye not that your body is the temple of the Holy Ghost, which is in you. …'[xiii]

Dear sister, I am feeling a kind of thirst to ascend yet more in belief in the personal presence of the Holy Spirit in my situation; and that, through revelation, not by imagination, thinking to comprehend the manner and means that it comes to be, which would be true idolatry.[36]

She accepts tests and trials as sent from God to purge her worldly desires, and believes that God can do this for the congregation at Pontrobert, which she sees at times as backslidden and in need of restoration. Her attitude is never

<hr>

[x] 2 Cor. 5: 19.
[xi] 2 Tim. 1: 12.
[xii] Phil. 1: 23.
[xiii] 1 Cor. 6: 19.

simply critical or judgmental, but rather longing for the restoration and renewal she believes is available when people turn back wholeheartedly to Jesus Christ. Ann recognizes the blessings evident in the fellowship, as well as the failings:

> We had privileges of great worth in recent days; we had the administration of the Lord's Supper twice, and a comforting fragrance on the breaking of bread.[37]

> I desire you especially to take the bride of the lamb to the throne of grace; groan much for her restoration; commend her to her bridegroom.[38]

> It is a dark time at present for the church in Pontrobert.[39]

> That word is much on my mind and others too as I look upon her feeble, slovenly and disheartened appearance, 'Is this Naomi?'[xiv] [40]

> The poor state of the cause of God in a number of places these days presses grievously on my mind.[41]

the Old Chapel, Pontrobert

[xiv] Ruth 1: 19.

But there is always hope:

> I took great pleasure one night confronting these things as I thought what the Holy Spirit says of the church; two passages of scripture were on my mind, 'Glorious things are spoken of thee, O city of God';[xv] 'the Lord thy God is strong in the midst of thee.'[xvi][42]

These words from Ann show where her heart ultimately rested:

> I wish to say it with thanksgiving—that despite my whole depravity, and the devices of hell, the world, and the things within it, by the goodness of God alone, I have not changed the object of my love up till this night. But rather I intend from my heart to rest in his love, and to delight in it, always singing, though I shall not attain to it this side of death even to the least degree to encourage me, except through strife.[43]

> I can say that it is this that cheers my mind more than anything these days; not dying itself, but the great gain that is to be gained through death; to be able to lay aside every inclination to dishonour the law of God, every weakness being swallowed up by strength, to obtain complete conformity with the law, which is already the desire of my heart, and to enjoy the likeness of God for ever.[44]

Three of Ann's letters to John Hughes close with Ann's sense of her mortality and of the uncertainty of life:

> This is from your fellow pilgrim journeying towards eternity.[45]

> I am your unworthy sister who is swiftly running to the world that endures for ever.[46]

> This is from one who journeys speedily through the world of time to the world that endures for ever.[47]

[xv] Ps. 87: 3.
[xvi] Ps. 46: 5.

CONCLUSION

WHAT IMPRESSION is left in the reader's mind by the hymns and letters of Ann Griffiths? Perhaps that the world in which Ann grew up is vastly different from the highly technical world of today, with its media and sophistication. Ann lived in a quiet rural backwater, where conversation and religion had a far greater potency than is usually experienced today. An intelligent young woman such as Ann had more time to meditate in quietness and to share her thoughts with her closest friends. Her awareness of her sinfulness—('depravity'; 'self-conceit'; 'spiritual whoredom') is the consequence of a life lived very close to the light of Christ, where the darkness of sin stands out more starkly.

It was supremely true of Ann Griffiths that she loved much because, as she believed, she had been forgiven much. In a profound sense, in the midst of all her turbulence of spirit, she found calm as she rested in the love of God revealed in and through the Cross of Jesus:

> Here we find the tent of meeting,
> here the blood that reconciles;
> here is refuge for the slayer,
> here the remedy that heals;
> here a place beside the Godhead
> here the sinner's nesting place,
> where, for ever, God's pure justice
> greets us with a smiling face.[48]

* * * * * * *

Ann's memorial in the churchyard at Llanfihangel-yng-Ngwynfa is beside the path leading to the church. A tall obelisk (paid for by public subscription) carries a simple inscription:

Er cof am Ann Griffiths

Dolwar Fechan

Ganwyd 1776   Bu farw 1805

[*In memory of Ann Griffiths*

Dolwar Fechan

Born 1776   Died 1805]

One may look out from the churchyard over a wide panorama, the quiet hills and valleys of Montgomeryshire with the high Berwyns in the distance, and wonder that such a remote, undisturbed corner of Wales produced such a distinctive and inspired a voice as that of Ann Griffiths.

Ann Griffiths Memorial
the churchyard, Llanfihangel-yng-Ngwynfa

NOTES

The translations have been taken from *Hymns and Letters, Ann Griffiths*, ed. & trans. by Alan Gaunt & Alan Luff, Stainer & Bell, 1999. ISBN: 978-0-85249-854-3.

[1] Published in the periodical *Y Traethodydd* ('The Essayist'), 1846.

[2] Hymn 30: Ever in a sea of wonders (*Mewn môr o ryfeddodau*).

[3] Hymn 31: Long ago, with Sinai blazing (*Pan oedd Seinai gynt yn danllyd*).

[4] Hymn 7: Though the soul in greatest fervour (*Pan fo'r enaid mwya gwresog*), v. 1.

[5] Hymn 11: I will walk the vale of weeping (*Yng nglyn wylofain bydd fy ymdaith*), v. 2.

[6] Hymn 16: The justice table of our God (*Ni ddaeth i fwrdd cyfiawnder Duw*), v. 2.

[7] Hymn 22: Wonder! wonder to the angels (*Rhyfedd, rhyfedd gan angylion*), Part 1, vv. 1 & 2.

[8] The set of thirty-nine doctrinal principles ('Articles of Religion') adopted by the Church of England in the second half of the sixteenth century as an accepted official response to the controversies of the Reformation. They are published in the *Book of Common Prayer* of 1662.

[9] Hymn 6: O for the faith, with angels (*O am gael ffydd i edrych*), v. 1.

[10] Hymn 1: Here we find the tent of meeting (*Dyma babell y cyfarfod*), vv. 2 & 3.

[11] Hymn 22, Part 1, v. 4.

[12] Hymn 12: See him stand among the myrtles (*Wele'n sefyll rhwng y myrtwydd*), v. 1

[13] Hymn 28: Must my zeal , like glowing embers (*A raid i'm sêl, oedd farwor tanllyd*), v. 1.

[14] Hymn 4: Though it crosses human nature (*Er mai cwbwl groes i natur*), v. 1.

[15] Hymn 9: O, my head should be all waters (*O na bai fy mhen yn ddyfroedd*), v. 1.

[16] Hymn 5: Comes the day the royal offspring (*Mae'r dydd yn dod i'r had brenhinol*), v. 1.

[17] Hymn 22, Part 2, v. 2.

[18] Hymn 32: In the waters of salvation (*Y mae dyfroedd iachawdwriaeth*).

[19] Hymn 3: Pilgrim, fainting in the tempest (*Bererin llesg gan rym y stormydd*), v. 2.

[20] Hymn 22, Part 2, v. 3.

[21] Letter 8 exists in Ann Griffiths' own handwriting. The others were copied, which may have included tidying up hastily-written notes. The translations are made from the texts given by Megan Siân in *Gwaith Ann Griffiths*, 1982.

[22] Letter 2 to John Hughes, 17 February 1801.

[23] Letter 1 to John Hughes, 28 November 1800.

[24] Letter 1.

[25] Letter 4 to John Hughes, undated.

[26] Letter 6 to John Hughes, undated.

[27] Letter 3 to John Hughes, undated.

[28] Letter 5 to John Hughes, undated.

[29] Letter 5.

[30] Letter 7.

[31] Letter 2.

[32] Letter 7 to John Hughes, undated.

[33] Letter 4.

[34] Letter 8 to Elizabeth Evans, undated.

[35] Letter 7.

[36] Letter 8.

[37] Letter 1.

[38] Letter 1.

[39] Letter 3.

[40] Letter 6.

[41] Letter 7.

[42] Letter 3.

[43] Letter 8.

[44] Letter 8.

[45] Letter 1.

[46] Letter 6.

[47] Letter 7.

[48] Hymn 1, v. 1.